Dancing with the Flame

~ poems ~

Jamieson Wolf

Talking with the Earth

Copyright© 2016 Jamieson Wolf

 ISBN: 978-1-928101-06-2

Cover Artist: Jamieson Wolf

Text: Jamieson Wolf

Wolf Flow Press

www.wolfflowpress.com

PRAISE FOR JAMIESON WOLF

"Jamieson Wolf is a gifted writer!"
Kelley Armstrong, New York Times Best Selling Author

"As I read, Jamieson Wolf taught me to dance to the beats of his heart. Tender, heartbreaking and beautiful."
Caroline Smailes, Author of In Search of Adam, Black Boxes, Like Bees to Honey and The Drowning of Arthur Braxton

"Jamieson Wolf writes like Augusten Burroughs without the cynicism."
Nasim Marie Jafry, Author of The State of Me

PRAISE FOR TALKING TO THE SKY and WALKING ON THE EARTH

"Expect the unexpected and be pleasantly surprised. Keep an open mind and heart and travel along with this author on a journey through life. Experience with him just what he has been living with and through this last year. I challenge you to change your thinking and attitude with this book. Bring on the adventure as you travel with him and get Talking to the Sky yourself."
Elaine Breault

I have had the pleasure of reading this collection a few times and will many more I am sure. Jamieson's words provokes the entire spectrum of emotions in his words, allowing feelings to surface in the reader easily. There is an almost haunting permanence in the stories he weaves, one that has taken me to my own experiences

that I thought were long lost. This poet is magical. His words are powerful and loving. A very very good read!!
Dava Gamble, Author of Silver Journey's and Silver Cusp

"With his unique style and powerful imagery, Jamieson Wolf lures us into this beautiful volume of poetry. Colors splash across the page, emotions are captured in a single word or phrase. We ride the city bus and see a woman's tears, feel the touch of a caring hand, experience the joy in a child's smile.

We walk a city street, hushed with snow. Friends and lovers meet with a warm breath on the cheek, a kiss, a sad goodbye. We witness courage, personal growth, moments of humor, strength, snatches of a dream.

Each poem is a stolen moment in time, raw, vivid, and intimate. Touching the Sky is an uplifting affirmation of life not soon forgotten."
Dianne Harstock, Author of Alex, Without Aiden and Philips Watcher

For Dianne Hartstock

A Note About Dancing with the Flame

"Talking to the Sky" was about finding my voice again. "Walking on the Earth" was about coming to terms with my life as it is now and the healing power of love. So what is the overall theme of Dancing with the Flame?

I often look at having Multiple Sclerosis and Cerebral Palsy as elements, as something that lives inside me and has physical form. I often feel as if I am playing with fire to some degree. Some days it's very hot to touch and others, it's as if the fire is inviting me to dance.

I chose to accept the invitation. I love all of myself, even the MS and the CP as they have taught me to be strong and what really, truly, matters.

So I chose to hold out my hand and continue dancing to my own beat. It's the only way I can roll.

There are a multitude of people who helped me along the way with this collection. Wonder Mom and Wonder Dad, thank you for being pillars of strength and courage for me. To the people who I hold close to my heart: my brilliant Writing Sister Kimberlee, the forever fabulous Alexandra, the amazing Meaghan, the awesome Karine and the courageous Dava. To the beautiful Pam, the lovely Nai, the wise and wonderful Sandy and the delightful Elaine. You all shower my life with love and sparkles and for that, I thank you.

Thanks go especially to Dianne Hartstock. From the very first poem I put out there into the world of cyberspace, she has been a champion for my words and a huge support of my poems. More than that, she inspired the title for this collection and I am so grateful for you.

I owe a huge debt of thanks and gratitude to Michael. Not only have you taught me what love really is, you continue to love me even when I'm trying to figure out plot lines or character motivations and are always a willing sounding board when I'm thinking out loud.

Thank you for loving me and for supporting not only me, but my craft. Words can't express my gratitude, nor the love I feel for you.

Jamieson

Dancing with the Flame

~ poems ~

Jamieson Wolf

A Man Remembered

There was a sea
of police cars in
front of my building.
They dotted the pavement,
their lights shining like
flowers caught in the snow.
Entering my building,
I saw a stretcher in front
of the elevators. It was
red and empty. I wondered
what had happened,
if someone was hurt.
I saw the Super standing
by the elevators, as if lost.
He looked unreachable.
I moved towards him,
called his name softly so
that he would hear me.
I had the sense something
was very wrong indeed.
He looked up at me,
hearing my approach.
"What's wrong? What happened?"
My voice seemed loud,
echoing off the lobby walls,
the lobby itself somehow
bigger than it was.

11

When he raise his eyes to mine,
they were red and swollen,
tears having dried upon his face,
marking his skin like ink.
"You know the man downstairs?"
He asked me. His voice was cracked
and dry, as if he had forgotten
how to speak. I shook my head,
unsure of who he meant.
"He wasn't well. Very paranoid. He'd changed his locks so
no one could get in."
I was silent, not sure what to say;
not sure there was anything
that could be said. The Super
let out a sound that was
part breath of release
and part sob. He took a
deep breath and I imagined him
swallowing the sob, as if
taking it back into him.
"I've never seen a dead body. People were complaining
about the smell."
I found my voice, a small
quiet part of it that slipped
past my lips
"Didn't anyone know him? Any family? Someone
must have known him."
The Super shook his head,
more tears sliding down his

12

face in the tracks left
by the ones that had dried.
"He didn't have anyone. He was alone."
The sob broke free then and he
turned away for a moment.
When he turned back, he was
more composed, holding it together.
"You always hear about this in the movies, you know? This
doesn't feel like a movie."
I nodded, my voice having gone again.
I needed to get away, to feel the
cool air upon my face.
As I walked out of my building,
I watched the blue and red lights
make patterns on the snow.
I breathed in the air,
relishing its bite,
grateful that I was alive
to feel it upon my skin.
When I walked back into my building,
they were bringing the stretcher
out of the elevator. This time,
it wasn't empty. This time,
the man lay upon it,
encased in a cocoon. It reminded me
of a red chrysalis.
I stood to the side as
other men took the man outside
and away from me.

I watched him go and wondered
why there was no one that
would find out about him,
no one who would miss him,
mourn his passing, no one
who would remember him
for the man that he used to be.
I gave the Super a final nod,
which he returned, before
going back inside my apartment.
Once inside, gathered some sage
that I had purchased.
I said a short prayer for him
and hoped that he could hear me.
**"I just want you to know that even though we never
met, I'll remember you."**
I took a breath then and
lit the sage, watching the flakes
turn into fragrant smoke.
**"You're free now. Free. So be at peace. I'll
remember you."**
As I watched the smoke
from the sage float towards the ceiling,
I pictured his spirit,
free from the chrysalis of his body.
I pictured his spirit.
He had finally grown wings
so that he could fly
home. I watched the sage

14

burn out.

"I'll remember you,"
I said.

You Have My Heart

I agonized over
what to get
him for Love
Day. It had
never been my
favourite day, it
had always been
a day of
heartache instead of
light. I commented
on this one
night as Love
Day was fast
approaching. He took
my hands in
his and smiled.
"You don't have to get me anything."
He said kindly.
"But I do. I have to find something for you that shows you
how much I love you."
He saw the
look of anguish
on my face
and smiled again.
"You already have given me something."
"No, I haven't."
"You have. Look."

He took my
hand and touched
it to his
chest. Under my
hand, a brilliant
golden light began
to shine forth.
"That's your heart. You gave it to me the first time you told
me you loved me."
I felt my
hearts warmth emanating
from him. He
took his hand
and pressed it
to my chest.
Gold light spilled
from beneath his
hand and the
light pulsated in
time with the
light that came
from his chest.
"If you have my heart, what's inside of you?"
"Don't you know?"
I shook my
head, seeing him
smile once again.
"It's my heart. I gave it to you the first time I told you I
loved you."

17

I was breathless
with want for
him at that
moment and kissed
him softly on
his gorgeous lips.
When our lips
met, our hearts
sang to each
other, filling the
room with soft
golden light

You Are Everything Beautiful

You are everything
that is beautiful
to me. You
are like the
sun that shines
above our heads,
the air that
rushes past our
faces, the water
that give us
life. You are
birdsong that inspires
hope, the grass
under our feet
that whispers our
dreams and wishes
as we walk
upon it. You
are the stars
themselves that we
wish upon. You
are my wish
I never thought
would come true.
You are everything,
all these things
and more. When

I think of
beauty, I think
of you and
what we have
together. When I
think of you,
I am filled
with light and
love for you.
You are the
embodiment of all
that is beautiful
in the world
and I am
so thankful to
be loved by
you in return.
You are everything
beautiful and whenever
I think of
you, I am
happy.

Believe the Impossible

I never believed
in Love until
I met you.
I believed in
the idea of
love, that two
people could meet
and something would
erupt into flame
inside of them,
from their kisses
or even the
simplest touch. I
looked high and
low and found
versions of love
but it wasn't
the real thing.
It was only
a facsimile of
what love was
supposed to be.
I resigned myself
to a lifetime
alone loving myself,
thinking this was
all that I

would have, all
that could be.
Then you came
into my life
and changed every
aspect of it.
You changed me,
filling my heart
not with hope
for something that
would never be,
but with love,
the love that
I had dreamed
of but thought
impossible to attain.
You make me
a better person
with you in
my life to
fill it with
joy, support and
with happiness I
never thought I
would ever experience.
You fill my
dreams with light
instead of darkness
and my waking

hours with thoughts
of you. Every
time I think
of you, my
heart pulsates with
a soft glow
that fills first
my chest and
then the rest
of my body.
When you kiss
me, a fire
spreads along my
lips and down
through my body,
lighting the candle
I carry for
you within me.
Thank you for
showing me what
true love really
is and that
dreams, however big,
however impossible they
may seem are
really just wishes,
waiting to be
granted.

Floating on a Sea of Stars

I walked into
the room and
tried not to
shiver. The hospital
was cold, especially
so in my
gown with my
back exposed for
all to see.
The technician smiled
weakly at me.
It was late
and who knew
how many MRI's
she still had
left to do.
She gestured to
the machine, sitting
larger than life
in the middle
of the room.
"Here are your ear plugs. And you even get a little party
hat."
She handed me
a disposable cap
that kept the
machine sterile. She

gestured again at
the MRI machine.
*"I want you to lay down, putting your head here in this rest.
I'm also going to prop a pillow under your legs."*
I nodded and
hefted myself up
onto the table.
I lay down
as she helped
me guide myself
into the proper
position. She attached
the camera that
would take close
pictures of my
head and neck.
This was the
moment I always
began to lose
it a little.
I felt I
was being shut
into a cage,
with no exit.
"Try not to move while the MRI is on."
She said. I
knew I would
be able to
hear her voice

once I was
in the machine.
I nodded and
the table slid
into the long
metallic tube. My eyes
were closed and
despite whatever bravery
I possessed, my
eyes watered with
a few tears.
I opened them
and blinked a
few times to
chase the tears
away. It was
then that I
noticed the stars.
Someone had stuck
stars on the
inside of the
tube. I looked
at them and
marveled at the
sight of such
a happy thing
here. I heard
the clicks of
the machine starting

up and then
the MRI started,
shaking the table
that I lay on
as the magnetic
rings moved faster
and faster around
me. I closed
my eyes and
focused on my
breathing. After a
few breaths, I
was able to
breathe deeply. I
eased into
my breathing, letting
their rhythm compliment
the sounds of the
machine as it
thrummed around me.
After some time,
It began to
feel as if
I was sliding
out of the
magnetic tube. I
opened my eyes
and saw the
stars were still

in front of
me. I hadn't
moved. I closed
my eyes again
and after a
moment, the sensation
of moving returned.
It was as if
an unseen wave
of water ran
beneath me, except
it wasn't water,
but stars. I
could feel their
sparkle caress my
skin. I was
still moving, sliding
out of the
machine. I heard
a voice speak
in my ear.
*"You're doing so well. We're almost done. Just a few more
minutes."*
I opened my
eyes and saw
the sky, filled
with sparkling stars.
They joined with
the ones that

held me aloft.
I floated there,
held by a sea
of stars. It
seemed like I
could look into
them forever and
never see the
end. Below me,
the machine began
one last loud
round of thrums,
bumps and beeps
It sounded like
the music that
stars would make,
unintelligible to my
human ears. The
the voice spoke
softly once more.
"You're almost done. You better come back now. You're
almost done."
I closed my
eyes and relaxed,
floating downward until
I felt the press of
the sliding table
against my back.
The tickling of

the stars lessened
as the machine
began to settle
itself around me.
I felt the
stars leave from
beneath my body.
They slide out
as if made
of water. Then
the machine gave
one final click.
I opened my
eyes and was
once more looking
at the yellow
stars that someone
had stuck inside
the machine. I
said a silent
note of thanks
to that technician,
as those stars
had given me
a way to
float amongst the
stars that came
from forever. As
I walked out

of the room,
I looked behind
me and saw
that I left
behind a trail
of stars, sparkling
in the air.
I almost reached
out to touch
them, to run
my fingers through
them. Instead, I
made a wish
on one of
them and hoped
that it would
come true.

The Light Inside of Us

Even as a
writer, I am
often at a
loss for words.
When I look
into your beautiful
eyes and see
myself reflected from
within, I tell you
that I'm grateful
for your love
and your kindness,
though that only
comes close. When
you take my
hand and the
simple gesture makes
me feel more
whole than I
have ever been,
I tell you
that I'm honoured
by your presence
in my life,
but the words
don't describe everything
I'm feeling. When

you tell me
that you love
me, I tell you
I love you
in return, but
trying to fit
everything into those
three words seems
impossible. Now, as
we embark on
building a life
together, joining our
lives into one, I
try to express
how thrilled I
am, how happy
you make me,
how you make
me a better
man. I can
only hope that
you know this,
that you can
feel the words
I want to
say but can
find no breath
large enough to
hold them. I

know that the
emotions I can't
find the right
words for thrum
within my body,
making it vibrate
with light. I
can only hope
that when I
take your hand,
and put it
to my heart,
you can feel
the vibrations of
words not spoken
and that you
know their meaning.
If I am
ever lost, I
know that all
you will have
to do is
follow the light
that you create
within me and
I will be
guided by the
light I create
inside of you.

Seeing Into Both Worlds

I see her
coming towards me.
She is walking
with a cane
but solders onward,
every step taken with
purpose. She looks
up and sees
me and I
feel as if
she is taking
stock of what
I'm made of.
She stops in
front of me
and we regard
each other for
a moment. Then
she speaks, in
a voice that
has known the
raspy embrace of
too many cigarettes.
"Look at me,"
she says, and
I do, I
am. She moves

her hand upward
and snaps her
fingers at me.
"I said, look at me."
I've experienced this
before. I sigh.
*"I am looking at you. I only use one eye at a time to focus on
people."*
"Is that a medical condition?"
"No, I was born this way."
She nods as
if this confirms
her thoughts.
"I thought so. You see into both worlds, then."
I'm taken aback
by her words.
"What do you mean?"
**"You use one eye at a time, right? What is the other
eye looking at when this eye is focusing on me?"**
*"It widens my field of vision. I can look ahead of me and
beside me."*
"So you travel the plains of both worlds."
I shrug, and
try to explain.
"No, it was just a lazy eye that was never corrected."
**"Nor should it. You haven't seen all you have yet to
see. Do you see goodness or duplicity in others, just
by looking at them?"**
I shrugged again.

36

"I just go with my gut reaction. "
She waved a
hand as if
waving my words
away from her.
"You have yet to see, then, but you will. You will."
She put a
finger to my
chest and pressed.
She looked me
in the eyes,
first the right
one and then
the left one.
"You carry light with you. Don't give it to those that don't deserve it."
So saying, she
walked on past
me. I watched
her walk away
for a moment
until a group
of people passed
in front of
her. When they
had moved out
of the way,
I looked for
her, but she

was already gone.

I Wish...

As I was walking home,
I saw a man with
the bluest eyes. They were
a dark and vibrant blue,
the colour of a sky after
a storm has cleared.
I had a flash from
my youth, a wish to be
other than I was,
to not look as I did.
I had always wanted
blond hair and blue eyes.
For reasons unknown to me,
this was what I identified
as beautiful. As I
walked away from the
blue eyed man,
I whispered over and over:
"I wish, I wish, I wish...."
I stopped there, however.
What did I wish exactly?
Though my life was not
what I thought it would be,
I was happy.
Though I did not look
like everyone else,
I loved myself,

every part of me,
even my imperfections.
If I changed one iota
of who I was,
or what I looked like,
I would not be on
the path I was on today.
My life would be
different than it was now.
It wouldn't be the life
that I was living,
but someone else's.
I was finally happy
inside my own skin
and content with the life
that I've been given.
So instead, I simply said
"I wish..."
and left it at that.
For to wish for something
is to invite the possibility
of magic
into your life.
As I walked home,
the air around me began
to sparkle and shine
and I knew that
I was already
magical.

The World of the Pen

I don't see the
world in the same
way others do. In
my world, there are
dragons flying overhead, soaring
through the clouds. In
my world, there are
flowers and plants that
talk to you as
you walk along the
path. Sometimes, they sing.
In my world, there
are fair folk. Some
are kind, helping you
along on your path,
showing you the right
way. Others would lead
you astray, into the
deadly swamps that await
those who have lost
all hope. Yet, there
are even more strange
sights to see, unicorns
and griffins, ogres and
trolls, battling it out
over something you have
said, or didn't say.

There are darker corners
that are full of
despicable people, capable of
the darkest of deeds.
However, for every person
of darkness, there is
one of light so
pure and so complete
that it never fails
to shine in the
darkest corners of my
world, for good must
always triumph over
evil. I stop for a
moment on the path
that I've been walking
upon when my Prince
comes up behind me
and wraps his arms
around me in an
embrace. He is warm
and wonderful, full of
the kind of light
that shines so brightly.
"What are you writing?"
He asks. I answer
as truthfully as possible.
"I'm not sure yet."
His scent envelopes me.

"I can't wait to read it."
I carry a smile within
me as he walks
away and I wield
my pen, mightier than
the sword, and wait
for the story that
wants to be set
free.

<u>When You Are Away</u>

When you are
away, I dream
of you at
night. You come
into my sleep
like the wind
and it is
a cool balm
on my skin.
When you enter
my dream, all
I can see
is the light
that emanates from
you, so bright
that I am
momentarily blinded by
you. In the
dreams, we are
hand in hand,
exploring unseen territory,
unknown places: great
expanses of sand
stretching as far
as the eye
can see, meadows
full of flowers

begging to be
picked, caverns and
caves or cliffs.
In my dreams,
we travel the
world together. When
I wake, I
still feel your
hand in mine,
your body next
to me. Though
you are away,
you are never
far from me
as I carry
you inside my
heart. When I
wake, my body
is filled with
light that chases
away the darkness
of night, though
our travels during
slumber stay with
me, clear in
my mind. When
you are away,
I lay down
to sleep at

night and wonder
where we're going
next.

<u>You Have Given Me The World</u>

From the moment
that we met,
my life has
been filled with
light. As our
love has continued
to grow, I've
changed. Now, instead
of hiding and
hoping for a
better life, I'm
living it. Instead
of wishing for
magic, I'm creating
it. Instead of
shying away from
all of life's
pleasures, I'm embracing
them. Rather than
shy away from
anything, I'm meeting
things head on
unafraid of what
will happen. Instead
of waiting for
life to happen
to me, I'm making

my life happen.
Rather than try
to change me
into something that
you wanted me
to be, you
accepted me as
I was, as I
am, embracing all
of me and
all that I
could be. You
believe in me
even when my
belief in myself
flags or wavers.
You love even
the parts of
me that I
didn't love and
now I see
myself in a
different light, through
a different lens.
You have changed
my life into
something so wonderful.
You have also
turned the world

from a mystery
waiting to be
solved into something
waiting to be
discovered. You've shown
me what true
love really is
and I'm a
better man because
of you. You've
given me the
world and I'm
eternally grateful for
your light. You
have given me
the world and
I can't wait
to discover it
with you.

An Ode to a Home

When I moved here,
it was really an
awakening.
I stepped out of
the darkness of the
basement apartment,
with small windows
and a view of
the alleyway.
It was small enough
that I could stand
in my living room
and, with arms outstretched,
touch both walls.
I nicknamed it
the bat cave.
I had wanted to
find a place that I could
hide in and I did,
for six long years.
When I moved to
the place that became
my home, it was like
stepping out of the darkness
and into the light.
I began trying to
find myself within its walls

and outside of them.
I embraced life again,
finding joy in
the smaller things.
The sunlight streaming in
through the windows,
painting and writing,
the smell of incense.
the fact that I had
a bathroom within
the apartment.
More than that,
I found joy within myself,
within my perfect imperfections.
I found the light again
that lived within me.
It was a small flame
at first, but gradually,
it grew so that my
whole outlook on
life changed. Slowly,
I became me again,
letting the shadows
of my previous
apartment fall away.
As the light touched
the shadows I still
carried with me, it singed
the edges until the shadows

were nothing but smoke.
When the final shadow
was gone, I was free
of everything that had
held me down and held
me back. The forest
of trees was still there,
but it seemed far more
beautiful surrounded by
so much light. As I
prepare to move into a
new home and begin
another chapter of my
life, I realize I didn't
just find a home here.
I found myself
and for that,
I will be eternally
grateful.

Two Halves, One Heart

There is a
legend that says,
once upon a
time, we were
two people that
shared a body.
Two heads, two
hearts. The Gods
got angry and
split us into
two, forever separate,
the soul grieving
for the lost
part of themselves.
Most of us
spend our entire
lives looking for
the other half
of themselves, the
missing piece of
who they are
and what they
could be. Some
don't even know
what they're looking
for, just that
they know something

is missing, that
there is a
hole, wider than
a desert or
the deepest chasm,
inside of them.
We spend our
lives looking for
that spark in
someone's eyes that
speaks of recognition
and puts a
spark within our
own eyes. Some
never find their
soul mate, they
never find the
other half of
their heart. I
am lucky to
have found both
of these in
one man, or
to have him
find me. When
he gave me
his heart, I
gave him mine
in return and

when they were
joined as one,
the skies themselves
sang out in
joy. My soul
sings out with
glee as our
hearts become one
and light from
within it shines
forth, lighting our
way ever forward,
the light growing
brighter with each
stitch of the
needle and thread
pulling our hearts
closer together until
it becomes one.

You Are the Gift

There was a
box sitting on
the table. It
was an ordinary
kind of box,
beige and plain,
but there were
markings on the
side, as if
if had travelled
all over the
world. I looked
at the box.
"What's inside?"
You smiled at
me and said:
"You'll have to open it to find out."
I pulled the
box closer, surprised
by how light
it was. I
shook it, hearing
nothing inside. I
looked at you.
"What's inside?"
You only smiled,
the facial gesture

brightening your face.

"You'll have to open it to find out."

So, carefully, I
opened the box.
Light poured out,
filling our living
room with gorgeous
light, brighter than
any sun. The
light didn't blind.
Instead, it only
served to make
you look more
beautiful. I
looked to you.

"It's beautiful. Where does it come from?"

You didn't hesitate
when you answered.

"It's my love for you, given physical form. I wanted to get you a gift and this was all I could come up with."

I sat back
in your arms
and watched the
light play on
the ceiling, chasing
the shadows away.
I thought back
to how I

was, what I
had been, what
parts of me
I had left
behind. I was
a richer man
for having your
love in my
life in body,
mind and spirit.
I looked at
you and kissed
you gently, softly.
"You are the gift."
I said quietly.
"I can't imagine any better gift than you."
The light from
the box grew
brighter as my
love light mixed
with your own.
We sat there,
entranced by the
glow of what
we had created
together.

Dance Across the Page

In the dream,
I'm talking about
my writing, about
the novel I'm
working on, the
poems that I'm
writing, the short
stories I'm bringing
to life. I
see myself in
the dream and
my face looks
so lively, animated.
I happen to
look down at
my feet and
see that, for
some reason, I'm
wearing dance shoes.
They are leaving
ink stains on
the floor as
I walk along
with my companion.
Then I look
closer and see
that the floor

is made out
of paper, that
I am leaving
footprints shaped like
words behind me.
I wake, only
for a moment,
wondering what the
dream meant. When
sleep finds me
once again, I
find myself in
another dream. I'm
talking to a
fellow writer about
the dream I
just had. I'm
looking at her
in bewildered confusion.
"I just don't understand what the dream meant,"
I tell her.
"I don't understand what it was trying to tell me."
She gives me
a look of
patience, as if
the meaning behind
the dream should
have been obvious.
"I think the meaning is pretty clear. You're a writer. You

can't keep your words bottled up. You have to dance across the page."
I wake with
a start, wondering
at the almost
dream within a
dream, at what
my subconscious was
telling me. I
feel the urge
to write, I
need to write.
It is who
I am.

Clouds and Spirit Wind

My mind is
full of clouds
and my spirit
is the wind.
The clouds are
shaped like you.
I can see
the outline of
your chin, the
strong set of
your jaw, it's
disapproving frown seeming
to mock me
as it did
so many times
before. Lately, I've
started to forget
you. The timbre
of your voice
when you got
angry, the colour
of your eyes.
What your middle
name was or
your birthday. Those
details ceased to
matter, though I

thought they would
be burned into
my mind forever.
The more I
forgot, the more
I was able
to let go.
As I look
at the clouds
inside my head,
they begin to
disassemble, the wind
of my spirit
growing ever stronger,
a storm without
lightning. I watch
the growing breeze
and wonder why
what you thought
of me mattered
so much, why
I've carried pieces
of you around
with me like
a hair shirt
made of needles.
Why I've based
my self-worth on
someone who isn't

worth anything to
me anymore; who
didn't treat me
like I was
worth anything at
all except a
convenience. I stare
at the clouds
as they continue
to shift and
watch as the
outline of your
face begins to
disappear, the shape
of your brow
begins to lessen.
Thunder from the
clouds that make
your shape and
form let out
a rumble of
thunder and there
is a streak of
lightning in my
head that flashes
sharp like a
knife. I take
a deep breath.
"I let you go."

I whisper softly.
"As I forget you, I let you go."
My spirit grew
brighter than a
star, shining brilliantly
upon the clouds.
It began to
gather force, creating
its own wind
to push away
the gathering storm.
The spirit wind
ran at the
growing mass of
darkness and pushed
the clouds away,
forced them to
break apart until
there was nothing
left but smoke
and vapour. I
looked up at
the bright blue
sky within me
and my entire
body felt full
of the light
that had always
been within me.

"I've let you go."
I said and
took comfort from
how free of
clouds the sky
was.

Body Music

I try to
think of my
body as an
orchestra. The musicians
are busy warming
up and getting
ready to play
something wonderful. I
listen to the
musicians warming up
all their instruments.
The pains
and spasms in
my body are
like music. The
twinges in my
shoulders? The percussion
section banging on
cymbals. The slow
throb of pain
in my legs?
They are but
cellos playing a
soulful tune. The
intense stabs of
hot needles in
my back? Violins,

playing aggressively. The
fatigue, pulling me
into sleep? They
are but flutes
touching notes that
lull me into
slumber. The temporary
speech problems? It's
the conductor getting
ready. The loss
of balance as
I try to
walk? It's the
audience taking their
seats. Something good
always comes from
something bad and
my pain is
really my body's
music, and my
body is a
symphony of sound
and colour. Every
morning, I take
a moment to
see what kind
of tune it
will play today.
I listen to

my body and
the music that
it makes, hoping
to hear something
beautiful.

When Two Stars Meet

When I was
younger, there was
a star I
used to wish
upon. I would
always be able
to find it
in the sky
as it shone
the brightest. It
was with me
through thick and
thin, guiding me
through my past
and present. I
would wish upon
it, waiting for
the dream to
come true. A
few weeks before
I met you,
the star vanished.
I would look
for it within
the sky, but
it was gone.
Then I met

you and the
first thing I
noticed about you
was your light,
as if your
body couldn't contain
all of it.
I wondered if
I had been
a star for
you within your
own sky, guiding
you towards your
future, towards me.
As I grew
to know you,
then to love
you, I wondered
what two stars
who were earthbound
would look like
from above and
how brightly we
shone now that
we were together.

Elemental Man

You are the sun to me,
bright like Fire.
Every time I look into your eyes,
my world is brighter and
filled with light.
You are the wind to me
Every time you speak my name,
it's like a soft breeze
caressing my face.
You are the Earth to me,
supporting me with each
step that I take.
You are water to me.
Every time you tell me
that you love me,
my body and soul are
nourished by you.
You are the Element
that brings all of me to life
and you make my Spirit
whole.

A Joy All Her Own

They greeted each
other like old
friends. They sat
in the front
of the bus
and I was
only a seat
away from them.
The woman spoke
first, the smile
on her face
giving joy to
her voice. She
motioned to the
man as if
he had already
spoken to her.
**"I'm on my way to see someone at the office that
runs the shelter. They say they might have an
apartment for me."**
Her eyes lit
up with undeniable
happiness, giving a
glow to her
dark skin. The
man across from
her was older

and kept readjusting
his ball cap.
He gave her
a toothy grin.
"You're on the way to get an apartment. That's fantastic.
I'm so happy for you!"
"Yes, well, I'm a little worried."
"Why, you should be dancing! I danced for an entire night
when the mens shelter found me an apartment. A whole
home, just for me!"
She thought about
it for a
moment before responding.
"That's what I'm worried about. There are one
hundred and forty of us at the shelter. I won't have
to fight for the shower anymore!"
She smiled at
this simple gift.
"Imagine that, not fighting for the shower!"
"Or the toilet. Or wearing flip flops to the bathroom!"
"Oh, won't that be nice."
She said, her
face filled with
childlike joy so
potent the front
of the bus
seemed to shine.
"I wonder what I'll do first."
She said happily.

74

**"I think maybe I'll make the bed. Won't that be
wonderful? Or maybe clean the place from top to
bottom."**

Her face crumpled
slightly and the
joy slipped a
little from her
face. When she
spoke next, her
voice was softer.

"I'm afraid though."

"Why are you afraid? You'll have a place all your own!"

**"That's what I'm afraid of. I haven't been alone for
so long. There has always been someone nearby,
sometimes too close."**

"Then you have to get to know yourself. This is a gift, a joy!"

I watched the
woman nod enthusiastically.

**"Do you live with anyone? Is there someone waiting
at home for you?"**

The man nodded.

"My fiancée."

"Oh, what's her name?"

"She hasn't told me yet. But she will."

It was then
that I realized
they didn't know
each other and
were just meeting

for the first
time. I wondered
why they would
just start talking
to each other
as if they
were old friends.
Perhaps they saw
the same spark
in each other,
the same otherness
that set them
apart from everyone
else. The woman
rang the bell.
"Are you getting off here?"
"Yes, you going straight to their office?"
"Yes, to be shown my apartment!"
Her whole face
smiled. Gently, the
man shook his
head as they
moved towards the
door. He held
out his hand
to the woman.
"No, your joy. A joy all your own."
Her face smiled
more brightly than

before and she
took his hand.
"Yes, my joy. A joy all my own."
The bus stopped
and I watched
them for as
long as I
could, before the
bus zoomed away
leaving the woman
and her joy
behind me, but
with me at
the same time.

Bus Guru

He sat on
bus in the
front seats. He
had his legs
crossed, and thus
he had three
seats to himself.
He had long,
shaggy black hair
and he wore
sandals on his
feet that were
falling apart. Even
from my seat,
he smelled of
something akin to
rust and dirt,
as if he
carried the scent
of earth and
grass with him.
His hands were
together as if
he was in
prayer. There were
a stream of
words coming from

his mouth that
I couldn't fail
to overhear from
my seat. I
leaned in a
little closer while
everyone else kept
as far away
from him as
was humanly possible.
"They say God doesn't exist, but I know that God is many
things, he's the ground we walk on, the clouds we walk
under, the sky they are painted on. He has many names, so
many names."
A woman sitting
closer to him
than I was
let out a
snort of laughter.
He didn't stop the
flow of words.
"See how they laugh at you, how they choose not to know
you. Even the most un-religious person must agree that our
home came from someone. The angels tell me you exist and
so you must, my faith is that strong."
He kept his
eyes closed, but
still managed to
look peaceful as

if he were
talking to a
friend. Perhaps he
was. Maybe there
was a link
between him and
a higher power.
The woman laughed
this time instead
of snorting. The
man turned his
head towards her,
though he still
didn't open his
eyes. He pointed
a finger at
her and she
almost shrunk into
her seat.
*"You are married to a man who you do not love. Love him
or let him go."*
She gasped and
put a hand
to her mouth.
He pointed to
a man sitting
behind the woman.
*"You are too angry. People are afraid of you. Let the light in
to chase the darkness away. Only then will you be happy."*

The man made
a sound like
he was clearing
his throat and
coughing at the
same time. He
turned his head
and pointed at
me. I wondered
what he would
say, what wisdom
I had to
learn, what God
or the angels
had to say.
He was quiet
for a moment
but then spoke,
ever so softly.
"Sparkle on."
He said. It
was as if
the whisper came
from someone else,
sounding different than
his normal voice.
I wondered if
one of the
angels spoke through him.

"Sparkle on."

Who I Had Become

I hadn't been
through the suitcase
for some time.
It had sat
forgotten in my
storage locker. I
unzipped it and
found many forgotten
items. Among them
was an engagement
ring that a
man from my
past had given me.
Its shine
was gone, its
lustre dimmed. I
did not remember
who I had
been when he
had placed the
ring on my finger.
I could picture
him though: a
little lost, afraid,
surrounded by people
in the bar
where he had

given his proposal.
There was never
any question in
his mind that
I would accept.
I wore the
ring but after
only a little
time, it felt
too tight, as
if it was
burning my skin.
This was not
a fear of
commitment, but only
what I would
become when I
was wedded to
him. I remember
one of the
first things he
said when meeting
me face to
face for the
very first time.
"Well, you can stand to lose a little weight, you're quite fat.
I'll design a workout for you though."
There were no
terms of endearment,

84

only criticisms. He
would look at
me after I
had said something
off the cuff.
"Oh, my little freak. Who's my little freak?"
As I came
to know him,
I realized how
little we had
in common, how
little we had
to talk about.
"Why do you read so much? Would you please put down the
book and stop ignoring me?"
That was his
constant bitter refrain.
"What joy can there be in books, my little freak?"
When I found
the ring, all
this came rushing
back to me,
condensed into a
single memory, as
if there was
a time lapse
camera inside of
my head. I
saw who and

what I had
been. It was
made even more
clear to me
what I had
become. I was
stronger, I was
more whole and
made complete by
the love of
a man who
loved me unconditionally,
who loved everything
about me, who
cherished every thing
that made me
all of who
I was. I looked
at the ring
with no remorse
for what had
transpired, no hate
towards that man,
nor did I
hate who I
had been. Instead,
I looked at
the ring and
said, softly:

**"Thank you for showing me that I was worth more.
Thank you for showing me what I didn't want.
Thank you for showing me that I was stronger than I
thought I was."**
Then I let
the ring fall
from my fingers
into the trash,
along with who
I had been.
I turned away
and instead focused
on who I
had become.

The Scent of Ink

I walk inside
myself until I
reach its resting
place. It looks
as it always
has, timeless but
aged nonetheless. I
run my hand
along its stone
rim, feeling its
warmth. I hear
the voices whispering.
I look down
into the darkness
of the well.
It smells of
water and salt
and something more.
There is a
scent of potential
in the air,
something waiting to
be described, to
be detailed on
the page. I
never know where
my mind will

go or where
it will pull
the stories from,
but they all
come from here.
They all come
from the well
inside of me.
Sometimes, the water
level is quite
high, the stories
and voices pouring
forth so quick
that all I
have to do
is hold the
page so that
it can catch
the droplets. Other
times, the water
level is lower
and I have
to use the
wooden bucket that
is secured by
a thick rope
to gather the
water within it.
This is one

of those times.
I start to
lower the bucket
gently downward, trying
to place the
scent. It's not
brick or mortar,
nor grass or
soot. It is
something thicker, with
more substance. It
reminds me of
what wishes would
smell like, if they
had a scent.
The bucket hits
the water and
I feel the
rope pulling taut.
As I begin
to pull the
bucket up, the
scent grows stronger
until it is
all I can
smell. Something clicks
within me and
I know the
scent. It is

indeed the perfume
of wishes. It
is the scent
of ink, waiting
to be shaped
upon paper into
words, into story,
into being. As
I pull the
bucket even higher,
I can hear
the voices of
characters I have
yet to write
speaking softly to me.
"Keep going, you're almost there. Almost there."
I give one
final pull on
the rope and
bucket is on
the edge. It
teeters for just
a moment, almost
righting itself, but
then it topples,
spilling all over
the ground. Where
it hits, waters
and plants begin

to grow, and
the land is
no longer barren
I feel the
water, the ink,
surging within, waiting
for me to
shape the ink
into places, into
people, into being.
I open my
eyes and sit
back, inhaling deeply,
the scent of
ink strong within
me.

The Forever Home

We were nearing
the end of
the Forever Forest.
Sunlight was starting
to pour through
the tree tops
and it left
diamond shaped shadows
on the ground
all around us.
My hand was
still clasped firmly
in yours, it's
warmth bringing me
comfort. I watched
the Forest change
around us as
we neared its
end. Gone were
the shadows that
had been ever
present, absent were
the dark creatures
that used to
fill the
branches. Instead, there
was only the

whisper of the
wind as it
moved through the
leaves, sounding
as if the
trees themselves were
whispering at us.
"What do you think we'll find when we leave the
forest?"
I asked. You
turned to me
and said simply:
"We'll have to see."
At the very
edge of the
forest, on the
top of the
highest branch, on
the very last
tree that graced
the path, a
black bird sang
to us. As
we watched it,
yellow feathers began
to sprout from
amongst the black
until the bird
was no longer

black, but a
brilliant shade of
gold. I looked
at you, confused.
"What's happening?"
"Don't you know? You've changed, so the forest must change,
too."
As we moved
past the tree
and out of
the forest completely,
the wind increased
and I heard the
cracking of wood,
and the bending
of branches. I
turned around, my
hand still clasped
in yours, and
watched the trees
change and morph
before us. The
burnt black bark
of the trees
began to flake
away, filling the
air with what
looked like soot.
As the pieces

of bark fell
through the air,
they, too, changed.
They began to
shimmer and pulse.
It took me
a moment to
realise that the
pulses followed the
beats of my
own heart. Everywhere
a piece of
bark fell, a
flower grew up
out of the
ground, quickly, as
if it were
thirsty for air.
Soon, the forest
floor was covered
with them. I
laughed out loud
to see such
brightness in a
place that had
held me prisoner
for so long.
"It's beautiful."
I said softly.

"So are you,"
you replied. The
heat that ran
through my body
whenever I thought
of you intensified
and for a
moment we both
glowed as bright
as stars. We
walked a little
further, into a
meadow filled with
grass and trees.
It astounded me
that, just beyond
the Forever Forest,
there had been
such beauty, just
waiting to be
found, but I
had been to
lost amongst the
shadows to see
anything. Standing in
the centre of
the meadow was
one tree, still
blackened. I wondered

at its placement
so far from
the forest, and
amongst such beauty
as the meadow.
**"Why is this here? Why isn't it back there with the
rest of the trees?"**
You looked at
it for a
moment and thought.
Then you said:
*"Even in light, there is darkness. As in darkness, there is
light."*
We walked nearer
to it. Up
close, we saw
that it wasn't
blackened by soot,
instead, the tree
was made from
what looked like
a black stone.
"It looks like black onyx,"
I said. Nervously,
I approached the
tree and ran
my hands along
its trunk. My
fingers saw two

similar shaped grooves.
I pointed them
out to you
and you came
closer to me.
"They look like handprints."
You said. I
nodded and put
my hand in
one of them.
Nothing happened. I
looked at you.
**"Maybe we both have to place our hands on the tree
at the same time?"**
I said. You
nodded and placed
your hand in
the second indentation.
Still nothing happened.
Then I had
a thought that
went off inside
my head like
a brilliant light.
I reached out
and took hold
of your other
hand. The moment
our hands were

connected, the tree
and the air
around it began
to hum. The
song-like noise grew
louder until the
very air around
the tree began
to vibrate and
glow
with its own
inner light. We stood
back and watched
as the tree
began to shift
and change shape,
morphing into something
new. It became
a curved archway
and I could
smell different scents
coming from it,
could hear noises
of people, strange
sounds so unknown
yet so familiar.
When the archway
was done shaping
itself into its

new form, there
was a blast of
light that was
warm on our
faces. Then it
was still. We
looked through the
archway and saw
a new path,
leading towards what
looked like a
great mansion, a
house that stood
empty but even
from where we
stood, I knew
it was lonely
for someone to
live within it.
"It's waiting for us,"
I whispered. Beside
me, you nodded
and squeezed my
hand. I turned
and stood on
my toes to
kiss you, trying
to communicate everything
into that kiss.

When I pulled
away, I saw
we were both
glowing once more.
You took my
hand and smiled
happily at me.
"Our forever home awaits."
You motioned at
the archway and
the house that
waited for us.
"Shall we?"
"We shall."
When we stepped
through the archway,
the forest, that
had held me
for so long,
let out a
chorus of birdsong.
It was the
most beautiful feeling
in the world
to me, outshone
only by my
love for you
and your love
for me.

Princess Taking Flight

She sat down
beside me, her
purse hitting my
knee. She glanced
over at me
and smiled brightly.
"Oh, I am sorry. You know women and their purses."
I was uplifted
looking at her
smile. I pointed
to her purse.
"It's all right. It matches your walker."
The purse was
purple, the same
colour as the
streamers she had
dangling from her
walker. She smiled.
"Well, it is my favourite colour."
"Mine too."
We shared a
moment of happy
silence as the
bus stopped next
to a high
school. Kids got
off the bus

and another group
of them ran
by the window,
calling out to
each other joyfully.
"Oh, to be that young again. Not a care in the world."
"To have that freedom,"
I said. She
looked at me.
*"You know, when I was a little girl, I had this scarf. I would
tie it round my neck and then run."*
She gave a
reminiscent sigh and
patted my hand.
*"I used to watch it as it streamed out behind me as I ran. It
was as if I were flying. I felt like a princess."*
"You still are,"
I said. She
rewarded me with
the brightest, most
dazzling smile. I
blushed when she
patted my hand
again. She let
out another reminiscent sigh.
*"I remember how free I used to feel when I ran, with my
scarf flowing out behind me."*
She looked out
the window as

if she could
see herself there.
"That was my freedom,"
she said. Then
she looked at
me and instead
of patting my
hand took it
in hers.
*"Are you free? Do you have freedom? Do you feel like you
can fly?"*
I thought of
everything I had
in my life,
how I had
finally found love,
finally started coming
into my own.
"I am and I do. For the first time in my life."
She released my
hand and patted
it again, looking happy.
*"Oh, I'm so glad. For its only when you learn to fly that you
can truly see the world."*
She reached over
and pulled the
bell and waited
for the bus
to stop. She

stood and looked
back at me.
"You have a good day now. And remember to keep flying."
I watched her
get off the
bus and when
the bus started
moving again, I
looked for her
but she wasn't
there, as if
she had already
flown away.

Something Beautiful

Everywhere I looked, there was bleakness.
The skies were grey and overcast,
the air was heavy with moisture.
The people waiting at the bus stop
looked tired and worn out.
I looked around to see if
I could spot anything of beauty,
but there wasn't anything I could see.
Slowly, it became brighter. The sun
was fighting to break free of the clouds.
As the sun shone its rays
down upon us, everyone visibly brightened.
People smiled at each other, others
said hello. It struck me then
how much joy a bit of sunshine
brings to people, how beautiful
the light made everything.
I looked down at the puddles left by
the rain that had fallen
and saw something moving
within the surface of the water.
It moved away quickly but then,
as more people walked by,
it was back again.
I crouched down to see what it was.
I heard birdsong coming from the puddles
and, instinctively, cupped my hands and

let some water flow into them.
I watched the shape I had
seen flow across the surface of
water and blinked in surprise.
I blinked again when I saw
what I held in my palm.
A sparrow, tiny and slightly ruffled,
looked at me and I thought
I saw more of the water
inside of its eyes.
Seeing my curiosity,
it let out a gorgeous string of notes
and the birdsong seemed to echo
along the rays of sunshine.
It occurred to me then that
there is beauty all around us,
even on the most bleak of days,
if our eyes are open enough to see it.
The sparrow stopped singing momentarily,
as if it had been waiting for me
to come to that conclusion
and flew from my hand in a flurry
of birdsong and sunshine.

The Future and Beyond

Last night, I
found myself in
my old basement
apartment again. There
were a few
differences, however. It
was bright and
filled with sunlight.
I looked at
the ceiling to
see if new
lights had been
installed, but there
were none. Then
I noticed that
the glow came
from me. The
phone in my
hand rang. I
answered it swiftly.
"Hello?"
The voice spoke
softly into my
ear, its words
filled with smoke.
"You don't belong here."
I looked at

the phone, wondering
at it and
the glow that
came from me.
*"You left this place behind to find yourself. You can't find
yourself in the past, you can only look forward to what is
coming."*
"Who is this?"
"Who are you? Who do you want to be?"
I looked out
a window that
hadn't been there
before. I realized
at that point
that I was
dreaming. I
put the phone
to my ear
again, listening to
the man breathing
on the other end.
"I want to be free,"
I said softly.
There was a
soft click in
my ear. The
window whipped open
and I watched
as a storm

gathered in the
field beyond. Soon,
that storm transformed
itself into a
tornado of epic
proportions. The glass
in the windows
broke and shattered
like diamonds and
they floated in
the air around
me. I was
still clutching the
phone to my
ear. I heard
the man's voice:
"Sometimes, transformation can come from the unlikeliest
of occurrences."
The line went
quiet again and
I let the
phone fall from
my hand. I
watched the tornado
coming ever closer
and knew that
it would never
hurt me, that
this was a

dream. But what
would it do
to my thoughts,
my dreams, the
things I held
dear to me?
Would I be
the same? I
looked down at
my feet and
saw I was
wearing a pair
of ruby coloured
high top sneakers.
This was my
dream, I thought.
Right before the
storm and wind
took me, I
clicked my heels
together three times.
"There's no place like home,"
I said.
"There's no place like home."
Then the wind
took me toward
the future and
beyond.

A Castle in the Sky

We have built a castle in the sky.
Every day starts like a dream
with you by my side,
your body warm from sleep.
As I go through the day,
the dream continues,
thoughts of you filling
my head, heart and spirit,
making them all brighter and whole.
When I come home to you,
the dream continues,
as we converse, rhapsodize and confide
in each other, in what we have built.
When I go to sleep at night,
with you again by my side,
I realize that the dream that I've had
for so long is now a reality.
Dreams do come true, but when
they are brought into reality,
they are so much more wonderful.
You and the home we have built,
the love we have towards one another,
those were dreams before you.
Now that they are a reality,
I wonder what other dreams
can come true?

Believe in the Dragonfly

Though I was walking in the sun,
my thoughts were drawn to
the other day. I had seen the man
who used to be my husband.
It was odd, looking at him.
Here was someone that I had loved,
but now felt nothing for him.
Not a whisper or murmur of
affection, just an echo of
what was and what used to be.
I knew that I was different now,
no longer content to just exist.
I wanted to live, to connect
with the world around me.
I was living my best life,
the only way I knew how.
Still, my thoughts were drawn
to him, to what he represented,
to the time in my life that
he had filled, overshadowing
my own self. I knew that
I was different now, that I had
gone so far down the path
towards the sun that I didn't
recognize myself or who I had been.
I stopped at the stone steps
that led up to the bridge.

Looking down, I saw the word
Believe
etched there in black ink.
I stopped to look at the word
and when I looked up,
I saw a dragonfly. It came toward me
and stopped to perch
on my shirtsleeve.
I looked at it, at the stillness
of it as it perched there.
It as if we were regarding each other,
or the dragonfly was trying
to tell me something.
I knew that the dragonfly
was a very powerful symbol
of growth and transformation,
that seeing one is a reminder
to embrace the light and
let go of the dark. I looked
at the dragonfly and tried
to hear what it was telling me.
As I watched the dragonfly,
it flew up in front of me,
so that I could see it completely.
Then it flew down to the word
at my feet and landed on it.
Believe.
Whether it meant for me
to believe in myself or

to just believe in magic,
in something greater than myself,
it didn't matter. I looked at it and whispered:
"I believe."
A breeze sighed around me
and the dragonfly flew away upon it.
I watched its progress until I
could no longer see anything
but the bright sun.
Believe.

The You Tree

The seed was
planted when you
first said my
name. The seed
pulsed inside the
earth, yearning to
grow. When we
first kissed, it
was the breath
of life to
the small seed,
water rich and
pure. The light
from your eyes
when you look
at me is
the sun, giving
the seed all
the light it
could need. Over
time, the seedling
grew into a
sapling, shooting from
the earth and
erupting all over
with little buds.
Over time, as

our love grew,
so did the
tree. Leaves sprouted
all along the
branches and flowers
bloomed, giving off
your scent. The
tree grew stronger
on your love
for me and
was nourished by
my love for
you. Soon, the
tree could no
longer be contained
within me. The
branches have grown
beyond the barrier
of my fingers,
the trunk is
larger than my
torso, the leaves
and the flowers
grow from me
and fly into
the breeze, falling to
cover the ground
behind me as
I walk towards

you. Every time
you take me
in your arms,
a breeze swims
through the branches
of the tree
that you planted
inside of me.
The You Tree
continues to grow
as our love
does, and will
forever reach for
the sky.

Long Live the Heirophant

From the moment
I read your
words, I knew
that you were
a storyteller. When
I met you
the first time,
I saw light
around you, shining
bright and blue,
with a golden
tinge to the
light that emanated
from you. As
I came to
know you, I
learned from you.
You taught me
to be strong,
to search for
strength in myself,
to live my
fullest life. As
I came to
know you better,
I was reminded
of the Hierophant,

the embodiment of
wisdom and knowledge
given form and
shape. Rather than
accept the reality
around you as
it was, you
filled pages with
your writing in
order to better
understand yourself and
your place in
the world. You
wrote for the
sheer joy of
it, the absolute
bliss of it.
You have to
know that
you are such
an inspiration to
me, to everyone
who knows you.
Bard, storyteller, mother,
friend, family of
the heart. You
are all of
these things and
more. The deep

fulfillment that you
have found in
yourself inspires me
to shine as
strongly as you
do and my
life is so
much brighter for
knowing you.

Brighter than the Stars

I try to
tell you how
much I love
you. My words
are lacking, even
after all this
time. It's difficult
to capture the
emotions you stir
inside of me
in three simple
words. Saying
I love you
doesn't seem like
enough. I try
anyways.
"I'm so in love with you."
I tell you
and you respond
in kind. It
doesn't capture everything
though. It fails
to tell you
how much you've
changed my life,
how much more
amazing it's become

since you entered
it. I try again.
"I love you beyond words."
That almost works,
for aren't I
always struggling to
find a way
to tell you
how I feel?
However, I'm a
writer and words
are my art.
I should be
able to tell
you how much
you make me
feel, how I've
become someone I
always wanted to
be, thanks to
your love and
your support, your
kindness that shines
from you in
all that you
do. So, I
try once again:
"I love you completely."
That still seems

to lack the
way I love you,
how our love
continues to grow
beyond our bodies
and the fact
that I love
you with my
entire body, heart
and soul. In
the end, I
know that when
you look at
me, even if
I haven't spoken,
you know exactly
how I feel
and return those
feelings in kind.
When you look
at me, you're
seeing all of
me, every bit
of my heart
and soul. All
those words I've
been trying to
find don't matter.
All that matters

is you and
the love we
have for each
other, brighter than
all the stars.

The Chariot

I've been living
with stones of
the past weighing
me down. I've
been carrying them
with me for too
long a time.
Some are large
and made from
metal, others are
jewel bright and
catch the sun.
Others still are
made from wood
or glass. Each
of them is
covered with something,
an image that
represents that part
of the past
weighing me down,
holding me back.
The chains or ropes
attaching them to me
chafe at me, raise red welts
on my skin.
I stand on

the street, looking
to the sun
when I see one
approaching me. It
stops in front
of me and
I notice the rider.
He looks a
little like me
and holds the
reins to three beasts
that pull his chariot.
"Want to come aboard?"
He asks me.
"Yes, please."
He shakes his
head, the sun
glinting off of
his armor like
little bits of
light given form..
*"You can't go forward with all that weight. How do you
even walk?"*
I bristle slightly.
"I manage just fine."
He looks at
me and I
see something in
his eyes, something

familiar. He nods.

"Come on then, if you must."

He holds out
his hand and
helps me up.
The Chariot begins
to move, but
slowly, so slowly.

"In order to move forward, you'll have to let some of that go."

I look at
my weight and
choose the largest
ones, untie them
from me. Others
with metal cuffs
holding them to
me click apart
and they fall
away behind me
on the roadside.
We move faster
now, the Chariot
gathering speed. I
look at the
stones that are
left. They are
smaller but some
of them are

the heaviest. I
hold them up
to him.
"What about these?"
He looks at the stones.
*"What about them? You will either let them go or hold on to
them. Only you can decide to be free."*
I nod, almost
knowing what he
would say to me.
I release the
other ropes and
cuffs and the
stones fall behind
me, clattering on
the pavement. The
marks and burns
still remain, though.
"Those will go away in time."
He says, kindly.
*"For now, they will remind you of how far you've come.
Remember, we are not defined by our scars."*
We travel on
for a while
until I ask him:
"Where are we going?"
He regards me
and then smiles,
handing me the

reins. He begins
to fade and
something in me
feels fuller,
brighter. I finally
recognize him as
myself, the me
I dreamed of being.
"Forward. Go forward, don't look back."
When he is
completely gone, I
am holding the
reins and can
feel the bright
sun on my
armor, turning me
into a sun.
"Forward,"
I whisper.
"Forward."

You Are Missing from Me

When you are away,
I don't merely miss you.
I yearn for you,
for everything you
bring to my life
and the life that we
build together. I am
restless when you're gone,
unsure of what to do
with myself, I feel adrift
in a world which I used
to see one way, but you
have given me a new way to
see it, a different way
to experience it,
to actually live life.
When you are away,
I don't merely miss you.
I ache for you,
for your hand in mine,
to hear your voice in my ear,
the sound of your laughter
or the feel of your lips against mine.
Since we've met,
I've found the other half of me
that was missing for so long,
the other piece of me

shining bright like the jewel
that you are.
My life is so much brighter
with you in it and you've
taught me to truly shine.
When you are away,
you are missing from me
and my whole self,
all of who I am,
yearns for your return.

I Love You Because...

I love you because
you truly know me,
every inch and breath
of who I am and you
just love me more.
I love you because
you helped me grow
beyond who I thought I was
and into who I truly am,
who I was meant to be.
I love you because
you make my soul so joyous
that it is filled with laughter
and music that only we can hear.
I love you because
you don't just speak to me
with your voice, but with
you're entire soul
with every word and every touch.
I love you because
you fill my world with a light
that shines so brilliantly,
so brightly, that others
can't help but notice it.
I love you because
you complete me
and continue to leave me breathless

with wanting you.

Reaching for the Sun

Two years ago,
there was only
darkness. My body
had rebelled against
me, shifting its
shape into something
new and, at
the time, utterly
terrifying. It was
the unknown of
how my life
would become that
I found most
frightening of all.
I hid inside
my hovel of
an apartment, the
forest growing ever
closer, the trees
growing larger by
the day. In
the space of
a couple of
weeks, I could
smell only the
trees and soil.
I gave up

and lay down
on the forest
floor, letting the
earth overtake me.
In a matter
of moments, there
was only darkness,
sweet, blissful and
cool. I relaxed
to the inevitable,
what my life
was now. Slowly,
though, something started
to happen. There
was a tingling
sensation that started
in my legs
and began to
work its way
up my body.
I felt something
in my skin
escape my body
and it began
to twist and
turn into the
soil. I could
hear it whispering
as it found

its way. I
began to see
light, finding its
way through chinks
and holes in
the dirt. The light
was brighter than
the darkness and
began to chase
away the shadows.
As I watched,
the holes became
wider as if
the ground were
moving. I realized,
when I felt
the pull on
my legs from
whatever had found its
way into the dirt,
that I was
the one in
movement, rising toward
the surface. In
an instant, I
broke free, staring
at the sun
and taking in
my first breath

of real air.
I marvelled at
Its beauty, at
the warmth and
heat of the
sun, how nourishing
it was after
so long in
the shadowy dark.
I looked down
at my feet
and realized what
the sensation had
been. I had
grown roots and
had been planted
in the very
earth itself. At
the time, I
didn't know what
would be coming,
but I did
know that there
was really only
one option left
to me. I had
only to grow.
I had only
to reach for

the sun and
beyond, no matter
what came. I
was not who
I had been
but had grown
into something more.
I had only
to reach for
the sun and
continue growing to
find out what
I had become.

<u>Stone and Fog</u>

I look out
at the world
from inside of
a brain fog.
It is a
storm that casts
its shadow on
everything I see.
I try to
speak but my
tongue doesn't move
the right way.
Words are like
stones that fall
from my mouth,
uncoordinated and heavy.
I try to
gather them as
they fall and
arrange them in
some semblance of
order. I look
down into my
hands to see
the stones that
have fallen but
the fog is

heavy and they
don't make sense:
I an many than me symposium. I an younger than I knew.
I let more
words fall from
my mouth and
catch them. I
can feel their
warmth and they
pulse with unsaid
meaning. I try
to arrange them
in some order:
I an many than me symptoms. I am younger than I know.
The right words
pulse in different
colours inside my
mind, shining through
the fog. I
merely have to
get my lips
to say the
right ones. I
try once more,
pronouncing my words
slowly, trying to
speak past the fog.
It takes all
of my effort

to do so:
I am more than my symptoms. I am stronger than I know.
When the right
words are uttered,
they act like
a spell that
chases away the
fog. It dissipates
with a *wooshing*
sound that leaves
me breathless for
a moment. The
fog will be
back, I know
this. However, I
will be ready.

The Perfect Mess of Living

"I don't know where it comes from,"
I told her.
"This need for perfection. I'm far too hard on myself."
She looked at
me, her lips
pursed in thought.
"Maybe that's why you got MS,"
she said. I
looked at her.
"What do you mean?"
"Well, the MS is trying to teach you that perfection doesn't exist. That's why it was given to you."
I was shocked
by her words.
She spoke of
MS like it
was a gift.
I knew that
everything happened for
a reason, but
that didn't ring
true for me.
"I think you're over reaching,"
I said quietly.
"There's no rhyme or reason why a person gets MS."
She thought my

words over but
continued undaunted nonetheless.
*"Well, think about it. It's trying to teach you something. It's
teaching you that you're no longer perfect, that you have to
learn to live with that."*
I remained quiet,
changed the subject.
Walking home,
the conversation stayed
with me, words
trailing behind me
like a mist
as I tried
to make sense
of them. I
thought she had
the wrong of
it. The MS
wasn't trying to
teach me about
perfection or my
lack thereof. I
thought harder, the
mist gathering like
a summer storm,
filled with hope
and wishes. I
could feel it
sparkling behind me,

its touch on
my skin like
rain. I knew
that my life
was different now
and that everything
did happen for
a reason, whether
we understood it
or not. So what
was the MS
trying to teach
me? I felt
a tug on
my arm. Looking
behind me, I
noticed a being
made entirely out
of mist vapours.
He looked like
shadow given a
more physical form.
"Who are you?"
He looked at
me but said
nothing. The light
that sparkled from
him grew brighter
and in that

light, I saw
beauty, I could
see solar systems
and stars. The
shape let out
a sigh, the
sound of wind
during summer,
and floated back
into me. I
was filled with
understanding then. I
knew that the
MS was a
gift in a
way. It taught
me thankfulness, it
taught me strength,
it taught me
courage. It showed
me what all
of those were.
I resolved then
and there to
just breathe, to
live and enjoy
every day and
to continue living
my life, come

what may. I
made a promise
to myself: that
I would not
search so hard
for perfection when
it didn't exist
and to let
go of hurts
that didn't need
to be there,
to ease up
on myself and
embrace the perfect
mess that I was.
Everything else was
living.

The Gift of One Word

I haven't spoken
to you in
nineteen years. Though
you are the
other half of
me, the mirror
of my physical
self, words between
us are few.
They float along
the water between
us, trying to
find their way
to you. The
words are simple.
Words or phrases like:
I love you. I miss you. I want to know who you are again.
The words sink
in the water
between us,
your ports are
closed, as is
your heart. You
don't hear what
I have been
saying for so
long. My words

are but smoke
signals to you,
which you choose
not to see.
Finally, I heard
a fog horn,
blaring from your
shores. It was
just one word
flying across the
ocean between us:
Thank-you.
It was the
most you had
said to me
in nineteen years.
It was like
a rainbow, shining
across the sky,
from you to
me. If I
go another nineteen
years without hearing
from you, that
one word will be
gift enough.

Stone Pathway

Half of my voice has disappeared.
Those lost words
sit on my tongue like birds,
flying away even as I try
to speak them out loud.
As I begin the process
of learning the second language
I knew so long ago,
it's as if I am
putting down a stone pathway
so that the birds
can find their way home again.

How Many Lifetimes

I dreamed we
were in a
cabin. There was
a crowd of
other people and
those in charge
said to us:
*"You will be reincarnated into other bodies. You will not
remember those you knew before."*
I looked at
you and wondered
what it would
do to me
if I could
never see your
face again, never
hear your heart
beat. We knew
that the world
was changing and
this was the
only way forward.
Then the dream
skipped ahead and
I was in
a different body,
everything around me

foreign in this
new skin. I
heard a voice
speak out to me:
"Hello."
I turned and
saw you. Though
you were in
a different body,
an unfamiliar skin,
your voice set
off fireworks inside
of me. I
looked at your
face and, though
it was not
the same, I
could see you
within it. Despite
their assurances that
we would not
know each other,
we did. As
you came closer
and ran your
finger along the
jaw of my
new face, I
wondered how many

lifetimes we had
lived through together
that we didn't
remember and how
many more lifetimes
we had yet
to live.

Sending Light

It was a surprise
to see her. She
looked at me and
the smile didn't really
reach her eyes. She
told me how nice
it was to see me,
but the words fell
from her lips like
stones she was glad
to be rid of. She
asked me how I
was doing. I told
her that the appointment
went well, that I
had passed the baseline
they had set two
years ago, that I
was stronger than ever.
"I even stopped walking with the cane,"
I told her, proudly.
"Well that's just great."
It didn't sound great
coming from her lips.
"Meanwhile, I'm looking at a wheelchair."
I told her that
I owed her a

debt of thanks. She
had told me to
take on a regimen of
stretches and exercise, that
this would help the
fight against my body.
She smiled and it
looked as if it
were paining her to
do so. She let
out a throaty laugh.
*"I see a physiotherapist and they give me exercises. But I'm
a bad patient."*
We said our goodbyes
and I was glad
to be away from
her, from her gaze
that was filled with
steel and coldness. I
wanted to be out
of the line of
fire, at the daggers
she was shooting towards
me. I wondered if she
wanted me to be
as miserable as she
was. As I rode
home, I thought on
her behaviour. I couldn't

fault her for it.
Indeed, I remembered how
it was for me,
deep within that dark
forest, alone with my
anger and hate at
what I had become.
I made the choice
to drag myself out
of the dark forest,
out of the shadows,
and into the light.
It was not an
easy choice to make.
Much as I hated
my life then, anger
is easier. So I
understood her vehemence, even
though I was no
longer that way myself.
So I did the
only thing I could
do. When I got
home, I sat for
a moment and pictured
a bright, shining light
that pulsed with energy.
Then I pushed that
light away from me

and sent it towards
her, hoping that when
it arrived, the light
would show her the
way out of her
own dark forest and
chase away her shadows.

A Seed of Light

When I think of you,
I smile and something
miraculous happens. I am
filled with a light
that starts in the
centre of my chest.
It begins as a
small seed, one that
you planted there. As
it grows inside of
me, I begin to smile
and that smile releases
joy into me, filling
me with such bliss
at the mere thought
of you. It combines
with the light that
I carry inside myself
for you until I
can see nothing but
your face, shining and
gorgeous like the sun.
Until I can hear
nothing but your
voice, soft like the
wind. My love for
you spills out of

my body, as it
is impossible to contain.
When I think of
you, my entire outlook
on life changes, my
spirit becomes brilliant with
the love I carry
for you

Beautiful Outside as Well as In

I was sitting
in the middle
of the bus.
There was a
woman waiting to
get off and
she called out
to the driver
"I pulled the bell for the wrong stop. I'm going to Shepard's
of Good Hope. Can you let me off at two stops down?"
While she waited,
she turned to
me and smiled.
"I used to be able to walk a lot. I was an athlete. Now I can't
walk three blocks."
I didn't know
what to say
but words came
out of my
mouth anyways, as
if being spoken
by someone else.
"The body changes. Sometimes there is nothing we
can do but live with our memories but then make
new ones."
She looked at
me with kind

eyes and gave
me another smile.
*"I want to live beyond my memories. I want to be beautiful
again like I remember being."*
I closed my
book and gave
her a smile
of my own.
"You're still beautiful."
"No, I'm not."
She said, letting
out a laugh.
"Sure you are."
I told her.
**"Beauty comes in all shapes and sizes. I think you're
beautiful."**
She blinked as
if in shock.
"Do you really think so?"
I looked at
her: she had
greying hair that
was escaping her
bun, a pale
face from too
much time indoors.
She was wearing
jogging pants with
flip flops and held

onto a purple
coat. She had
obviously seen better
times, easier ones.
But it was
when she smiled
that she seemed
to transform. It
took years off
her face and
I saw a
little of what
she used to
look like.

"Yes. I do. You have a light inside you that shines brightly."
She put a
hand to her
hair and smiled
again and I
watched as the
light within her
grew beyond the
body and poured
out of her.
The bus stopped
and she looked
back at me
before stepping out

into the world
The light had
faded and I
looked at her,
a woman who
now looked younger
than her years.
"Thank you. I could probably walk a whole mile today.
That's the first time someone has paid me a compliment in
ages."
She stepped off
the bus, a
trail of light
following close behind
her, like fairy
dust or dreams
made real.

Dancing with the Flame

To me, she
has always danced
to her own
beat,
to her own
rhythm.
More than that,
through the kindness
of her spirit
that shines through
in electric beauty,
she inspires me.
When I read
what she has
written, it is
so real that
I can almost
picture the images
coming to life,
sprouting forth like
fire to alight
upon the page
causing her words
to glow brilliantly.
She doesn't merely
write but instead
dances with the

page. I long
to be so
free with my
words, so limitless.
I long to
evoke such beauty.
She shines like
a Princess of Words,
bright with the
joy of life
and filled with
so much passion
that it makes
the pages she
covers with her
words throb with
desire and wanting.
She makes me
want to write
more, to write
better and most
of all, to
dance and revel
in the freedom
of movement. My
hands itch to
slide across the
page and see
what stories I

can give light
to and what
will be chased
away in the
shadows.

Across the Sky

You came among us
already shining bright.
Slowly and with care,
you helped to encourage,
to shape and to define.
Now as you move on,
we are brighter and
more vibrant than before
because of you. We are
the galaxy and you are
the comet, heading towards
your future. You leave
a trail of stardust
behind you so that
we can chart your path
across the sky.

Heart Music

I was coming into
the lobby of my
building when one of
my neighbours stopped me.
"How are you?"
She asked with genuine
warmth. The smile on
her face was like
the sun on a
dark and dreary day.
"I'm doing fabulously,"
I said. She laughed
and the sound was
like wind chimes singing.
*"I have to ask you. I was passing by your apartment the
other night and heard the most beautiful music. What were
you listening to?"*
I ran through the
music I kept on
my phone, thinking she
might have heard some
of that. She shook
her head with each
song that I played.
*"No, it wasn't that. It was more melodious more ethereal.
Much more happy."*
She reached down to

touch one of my
legs. I heard music
playing in the air.
It was loud and
very harsh, like glass
being broken on pavement.
The string section was
all screeches and scratches
that sounded like knives.
"No, that's not it either."
She touched my head
and the music that
filled the air sounded
as if it belonged to
a dramatic movie, full
of cellos and sweeping
movements. She looked at
me with her head
tilted to the side.
"You're some sort of creative person aren't you?"
"I'm a writer. How did you know?"
"Because only a creative person lives with that kind of music inside them."
She went to touch my
chest I reached
out and held her
hands gently in mine.
"What are you doing? How are you making that music?"

"Why, you're the one making the music. Every part of the body has its own symphony, if you're quiet enough to listen for it."

She slipped her hands
out of my grasp
and placed them on
my chest near my
heart. The air was
filled with the most
beautiful music. Full of
harps and strings and
melodious wind instruments It
was at once beautiful
and mysterious as it
was like nothing I'd
ever heard before.

"There you are. That's what I was hearing. What were you doing last night?"

"I spent last night with my partner,"
I told her. She
smiled at me kindly.

"We weren't doing anything in particular. It was just enough that I was with him."

"That's heart music,"
she said. I looked
at her quizzically.

"What do you mean?"

"When the heart is most happy, that is when its song is the purest."

She went to go into
the elevator, but looked
back at me, smiling.
"You keep letting your heart sing, you hear me?"
I nodded and my
thoughts turned to him.
Already, I could hear
my heart starting to
sing.

Timeless

Every time I look upon you
it is like the first time.
When I wake,
I see the halo
that surrounds your head.
It twinkles like gold stars
and the stars rain down
upon you, surrounding me
as I lean in to kiss you.
Every time I kiss you,
it is like the first time,
filling me up with light
that makes me feel as if
I am filled with wishes
waiting to be granted
when your lips touch mine.
Every time you take my hand,
the same thrill runs up my arm,
and it pulses as our energies
entwine and combine,
filling me with light
that is brighter than
the light I carried when alone.
Every day with you
is like the first day.
Every moment with you
is like the first moment,

filled with anticipation,
infused with a wish that
entices the air with
stars and light
to grow brighter
and more vibrant.
You are timeless to me,
and though the love between us
is young, it feels like a love
that has spanned the ages,
stretching across time to grow
only when we found each other.
It's as if a seed was planted,
biding its time,
waiting to stretch
across the sky to fill it with stars
and stardust.
When we met,
that star was given the life
that it needed.
Now we are following
that glorious star as we
continue to grow and love
each other more every day,
throughout time and space.

<u>Shatter the Dark</u>

We are alone
behind our eyes.
Solitary inside ourselves,
the darkness is
total until we
breathe life into
thought and dreams,
until we shape
letters into syllables
and syllables into
so many words.
We shatter the
darkness that we
find inside of
ourselves until the
darkness becomes fragmented
and filled with
cracks. Through all
of those cracks,
we can see
light shining, waiting
to pour from
us in art,
in words, in
music, speech or
song. They are
the lights which

chase the darkness
away. When the
light shines strongly
enough, others will
be drawn to
it, others who
are filled with
their own kind
of light, so that
we are no
longer alone.

Climb the Mountain

Life is filled
with peaks and
valleys. I sometimes
wish there was
a way to
look out at
what is to
come, what hills
I will have
to climb and
what waits for
me at the
top of those
peaks, those mountains
towering over the
lower points. But
when I look
back at what
I've accomplished, at
the valleys I've
already waded across
and the hills
that I've had
to climb, I
wonder if I
would have done
anything differently. If

climbing those mountains
would have meant
so much to
me if I
had known what
was coming? As
I stand atop
the highest mountain
that I have
ever been on,
I realize that
it doesn't matter.
In life, there
are peaks and
valleys, mountains and
swamps, fields and
meadows, oceans and
lakes and more.
All that matters
is that I
keep going, keep
fighting, keep
dreaming. That I
keep on living
life to the
fullest, whether I'm
in a valley
or standing on
top of the

world. All that
matters is that
I keep going,
I keep climbing,
That I keep
breathing and finding
joy in the
smallest of things.

Peaks and Valleys

When I look
inside of myself
I am standing
on top of
a mountain. I
can look back
at every step
I have taken.
Each step is
marked with a
small white stone
and they shine
in the sunlight.
I can see
The dark home
I grew up
in at the
very beginning and
can follow the
line of stones
that shine like
diamonds. Along the
path are many
different forests. They
marked times in
my life that
were the darkest.

After the forests
come the hills,
when I was
climbing out of
the darkness towards
the sun. Interspersed
throughout, are bright
shining lights where
I was happiest.
I try to look
at what is
coming, what is
beyond, but all
I can see
are clouds and
a dark sky
filled with the
stars of possibility.
I know that
I have only
to wish upon
one of the
stars to make
it so and
embrace whatever comes
my way, knowing
that life is
full of peaks
and valleys, highs

and lows. I
look again, try
to see through
the fog and
stars and can
see only sunlight
of days yet
to come.

A Gift of Change

I was sitting
by the pool
when she approached
me. The sun
had gone down
and the darkness
of night had
come upon us,
lit only by
the twinkle of
stars, interspersed throughout
the sky like diamonds.
"Would you like a gift of change?"
She said to
me. I thought
that I had
misheard her. I
looked up into
her face and
found it full
of light despite
the darkness.
"I'm sorry? A gift exchange?"
She smiled again,
white teeth flashing
in the blackness
of the night.

"A gift of change,"
She said again.
"A Cuban gift, for you. Would you like one?"
I nodded and
she held out
a cup filled
with little slips
of paper. I
took one, choosing
it at random.
I tried to
give her a
peso, but she
shook her head.
"Change is free."
I looked at
the slip of
paper and saw
that it was
covered with words:
<u>A light Spirit, bright Soul, happy Heart</u>
I stared at
the words for
a moment, unsure
of what they
meant, what change
it was that
I was being
given. Then, as

Cuban music began
to play, sounding
as if it
were coming over
the mountains that
surrounded us, I
felt my soul
dance to the
sound, heard my
heart singing along
to the music.
As I sat
there, brightness began
to pour out
of me, spilling
from inside of
me, gliding from
my skin until
it joined the
stars in the
sky. I knew
that my soul
was at peace
and so was I.
Turning to the
woman to thank
her for her
gift of change,
I saw no

one there. Instead,
there was only
the glittering of
star light, dancing
along with the
music.

Magician of Magnitude

When I was
young, I thought
she was filled with
stars. She seemed
to light up
every room that
she was in.
When I was
a little older,
I thought she
was filled with
sparkles and fairy
dust, able to
make anything that
I wished come
true. When I
was older and
under threat, I
thought she was
filled with fire,
so fierce was
her need to
protect me. Now
that I am
even older, I
know she is
filled with magic.

Able to mend
a broken heart
with mere words,
capable of helping
a tarnished soul
with the simple
act of love,
able to breathe
life into the
seemingly ordinary and
make things magical.
She is all
of these things:
magician of feats,
conjurer of dreams
and most of
all, my Mom.

The Infinite Symphony

When I talk about you,
My thoughts are stars,
filled with wishes.
They rise up to the sky
so that everyone can
see how beautiful you are.
When I think about you,
my words are lights,
keeping away the darkness
of thoughts and acting
like lighthouses for
brighter shores.
When I write about you,
my words are like birds
as they fly across the page,
filling it with such emotion
that my words come to life.
When I look at you,
my heart sings a song
that only you can hear,
the notes appearing
in the air between us,
the tempo rising
as you hold me close.
The notes create a symphony,
each note played along my body,
until my entire world is filled

with the song of you,
filling the infinite
and beyond.

Yuletide Star

When I think
back on Yuletide
from my past,
I remember this
light that sat
above the tree
in the shape
of a star.
However, when I
took the star
down to grab
hold of that
light, it would
elude me, still
dancing away from
my grasp. I
would see it
as I walked
out in the
snow, dancing in
front of me,
as if leading
me towards something.
I would see
that light throughout
my life, always
dancing away from

me, as if
if wasn't time
yet for me
to be graced
by its presence.
When I
met you, the
first thing I
noticed was the
light that surrounded
you, the brightness
of your spirit,
and the glow
of your kindness
that emanated from
you, pulsing brightly
to the sound
of your voice.
I've realized that
the light I
followed all throughout
my life was
leading me to you.
It occurred
to me that
the light I
kept chasing after
as a child
and through out

my adult years,
was the light
that came from
you, for you
are that light,
that brightness and
this Yuletide, I
am thankful for
you.

The Princess of Disks

When I first
met her, I
thought she was
a wood nymph.
She stood with
the sun at
her back so
that she glowed
a brilliant golden
colour. When she
spoke, it was
softly and with
a mischievous smile.
"I hear you like Bjork."
She stepped forward
out of the
sunlight and, for
a moment, I
thought she held
a staff and
shield, that the
light from the
sun was actually
coming from her.
Then I blinked
my eyes and
the image was

194

gone. Throughout the
years though, that
image has returned,
time and time
again. She is
the epitome of
generosity and kindness,
always giving to
those that need
it. She is
considerate and kind,
oftentimes giving more
than she has.
More than that,
I have watched
as she creates
possibilities for herself,
as she ends
one cycle and
begins another one
anew. She directs
her power where
she needs to,
whether it be
to help others
or to lend
a hand whenever
one is needed.
Now, when I

think of her,
I see the
sun again, shining
so brightly and
brilliantly, that you
can't help be
awed by it
and by her.

The Beginning of Goodbye

I thought I
would feel sadness
or discontent. I
thought I would
be depressed or
sad that part
of my life
had ended here.
However, all I
experienced was a
sense of rightness,
the thrum of
gratification running though
my veins. I'm
not sure, but
I was probably
glowing. I got
the papers stamped
and paid my
fee. I expected
to feel sadness
but there was
only this overwhelming
sense of relief.
Too long I
have waited to
feel something other

than resentment or
despair when I
thought of him.
Now I was
filled only with
joy and peace
of my own making.
It was only
the first step,
but it is
that first step
that is the
most difficult,
the most frightening.
The first step
looks down from
a cliff, high
up in the
air. I had
two choices. I
could cower at
the top of
that cliff as
I had done
for years, or
I could take
the leap of
faith and trust
that my wings

would save me.
Instead of waiting
for him to
do the right
thing, I did
it myself. I
took the power
away from him
and made it my own.
My life is
mine to live
and I choose
to live it,
to embrace it,
whatever it may
bring. It is
the beginning of
goodbye for us,
but I'm so
much better without
him and will
be even better
when I'm not
carrying the shards
of what was
around with me.
Instead of carrying
those shards of
a chalice always

with me, I
take those shards
and fashion something
from them so
that rather than
cause me pain,
instead they capture
the sun, shining
light upon all
in my life
that is beautiful.

On the Road of Yellow Brick

She wakes within
the dream to
find herself in
an expanse of
green. A field
of grass stretching
for as far
as the eye
can see. Along
the grass, there
is a road
of bricks, coloured
in a bright
yellow hue. The
colour is impossibly
brilliant, as is
the green of
the grass. It
is as if
the colour here
is magnified by
the sun. She
looks up at
the sky and
sees a bright
orange sun, three
times as big

as the sun
she sees at
home. Looking down
at the road
of bricks again,
she sees a
man standing on
the path, smiling
at her in a
gentle sort of way.
"Where am I?"
She asks, uncertain.
"Well, where did you want to be?"
The man says.
He has dark
hair that looks
to be made
of leaves. He
shrugs and she
sees hay fall
out of the
collar of his shirt.
"It's hard to know where you're going if you don't know
where you are."
She nods, even
though she has
no idea what
to say.
"I want my life back. I want it as it used to be."

The straw man
gives her another
kind smile and
his words are
soft and comforting.
"Well now, I wouldn't want that. If you went back to the way you used to be, you wouldn't be who you are meant to be."
She shook her
head, the uncertainty
deepening, the unease
she carries with
her in the
waking world alive.
"I don't follow you. I just want to be normal again."
The straw man
waves his hand.
"Pshaw! Normal. What is normal? Normal is boring. Normal is a bowl of porridge without brown sugar. Normal is what you want, but it's not what you thirst for."
She nodded, seeing
truth in his words.
"I suppose you're right. I know I'm not like everyone else."
"You're special, Kimberlee. So very special. You have a light in you that shines brightly for all to see it. We are drawn to you like butterflies to the sun. You wouldn't have that light if you were normal."
The light that

he mentioned
begins to glow
from within her,
as if she is
carrying the sun
within her. She
watches the glow
intensify, even as
the light from
it makes the
road and the
straw man start
to fade away.

"Wait! What do I have to do? What can I do? How do I move forward?"
Even though the
man of straw
was fading from
sight, she could
see him smile.
"What you've always done. Keep putting one foot in front of the other. Keep shining and keep living you life to the fullest. Everything else will fall into place. Trust yourself."
"But why is it so difficult to do?"
"It's always harder for people like us. You are a bright, beautiful spirit. You will find your way and then the journey on the road of yellow brick will become a joy instead of a hindrance. Trust yourself,"
he said again.

204

Then the light
that was glowing
from inside of
her grew even
brighter and she
knew the dream
would fade away.
But she knew
that when she
woke, she would
have a brighter
sense of self
and the life
that was hers.
And from that
she drew comfort.
She looked forward
to the next
step she would
take along the
road of yellow brick.

What I Had Become

When the New Year began,
I looked into the mirror.
I saw a reflection of myself
from long ago. I was
lying on a bed, weak,
my whole world changed.
I watched as my reflection
lifted a hand and beckoned to me.
"Come on."
He said.
I touched a hand to the glass
and it was as if
there was no glass there.
The veil between the present
and the past was thin.
I stepped through the mirror
and found myself in a place
that I remembered but fought
so hard to forget.
It was dark and there was only
one small light in the room.
Even so, by that light I saw
who I used to be lying
on the bed, my past self,
my other self. He regarded me,
and I looked at him.
I remembered that day,

how the night before the New Year
my life had changed forever,
never to be the same again.
I knew just how he was feeling
as I had been him, he had been me.
He was weak and disoriented,
unable to walk very well at all,
his whole world seeming to
move around him, unable to keep still.
He regarded me with tired eyes,
the fear in them so total.
He knew that something was wrong.
"You forgot about me."
He said.
"You forgot our anniversary."
It was true. I had forgotten.
Every year since that day,
I always wondered if this
would be the year that it happened,
the year where I lost control
of my body once more.
For a while, I lived in fear
of December 31st, of who I had been
and of what I had become on that day.
"I'm sorry,"
I said.
"I did forget. I did forget you."
"Why?"
He asked.

"Because I left you behind. Because I'm so much stronger now. So much happier."
He regarded me with a blank expression,
the fear increasing in his eyes until
they were full of tears.
"I don't know what's wrong with me. I'm so afraid."
"I know,"
I said kindly.
I sat on the bed beside him and took his hand
in my own. It was cool and sweaty and
I remembered how warm I'd been,
how nothing had felt right,
and how my own body had turned against me.
"You'll have to be strong,"
I said.
"There is a lot more pain coming, but you'll have to be stronger than you've ever been. Can you do that for me?"
"I don't know how."
"You don't, but you'll learn. There will come a moment when you'll want to quit, where you'll want to give up and head towards the darkness. But I promise you, good times are coming."
He looked at me with such
an open expression, one of yearning
for something better. I remembered
wearing that look, wishing and hoping
so fiercely that it was painful.
"Okay,"

he said.

"Okay."

I heard my partner calling me from
the other side of the mirror,
his deep voice making the liquid glass
move in ripples. I took one last look
at who I used to be and patted his hand,
leaned forward to kiss him on the forehead.

"I have to go now."

"I know you do. Don't forget me, okay?"

"I won't, I promise."

With that, I stood and moved towards the glass.
When I stepped through the glass,
I left behind what I had been
and into what I had
become.

About the Author

Jamieson is an award winning, author of over forty books including the Number One Best Sellers, "Talking to the Sky" and "Walking on the Earth."

He is also an accomplished artist. He works in mixed media, charcoal, pastels and oil paints.

He currently lives in Ottawa, Ontario, Canada with his cat, Tula, who is fearless.

Learn more about Jamieson at www.JamiesonWolf.com

www.ingramcontent.com/pod-product-compliance
Lightning Source LLC
Chambersburg PA
CBHW071528040426
42452CB00008B/928